PITTSBURGH
PIRATES
STARS, STATS, HISTORY, AND MORE!
BY K. C. KELLEY

Published by The Child's World®
1980 Lookout Drive • Mankato, MN 56003-1705
800-599-READ • www.childsworld.com

ISBN 9781503828353
LCCN 2018944849

Printed in the United States of America
PAO2392

Photo Credits:
Cover: Joe Robbins (2)
Inside: AP Images: Harry Harris 17, Keith Srakocic 19;
Dreamstime.com: Landon Fitz 12, Jerry Coli 29; Library
of Congress: 8; Newscom: Quinn Harris/Icon DJI 4, Chris
Lee/TNS 27; Joe Robbins 7, 11, 14, 22, 25; Shutterstock:
Alice Mary Herden 21.

About the Author

K.C. Kelley is a huge sports
fan who has written more
than 100 books for kids. His
favorite sport is baseball.
He has also written about
football, basketball, soccer,
and even auto racing! He lives
in Santa Barbara, California.

On the Cover

Main photo: First baseman
Josh Bell
Inset: Hall of Fame hero
Roberto Clemente

CONTENTS

GO, PIRATES!

Real-life pirates go after treasure. The Pittsburgh Pirates want to win championships! The Pirates are one of the oldest teams in baseball. Their fans have been very patient—the team has not won a lot of titles. The Pirates played in the first **World Series** in 1903 . . . but not many since! The fans have stuck with their favorites, though! Can the Pirates capture the **pennant** again? Let's meet the Pirates!

◄ *Ivan Nova is a key part of the Pirates pitching staff.*

WHO ARE THE PIRATES?

The Pirates play in the National League (NL). That group is part of Major League Baseball (MLB). MLB also includes the American League (AL). There are 30 teams in MLB. The winner of the NL plays the winner of the AL in the World Series. Pirates fans are devoted to their team. They have gone a long time without a championship. Will it come soon?

Slugger Josh Bell heads for the plate after smacking another home run. ➤

WHERE THEY CAME FROM

A team called the Pittsburgh Alleghenys joined the NL in 1887. They got that name from a river that flows through the city. In 1891, the team changed its name to the Pirates. They have played in Pittsburgh ever since. The team used to play in the NL East. In 1994, they switched to the NL Central Division.

◄ *Hall of Famer Honus Wagner played for Pittsburgh from 1900 to 1917. He led the NL in batting eight times!*

WHO THEY PLAY

The Pirates play in the NL Central Division. The other teams in the NL Central are the Chicago Cubs, the Cincinnati Reds, the Milwaukee Brewers, and the St. Louis Cardinals. The Pirates play more games against their division **rivals** than against other teams. In all, the Pirates play 162 games each season. They play 81 games at home and 81 on the road. The Pirates play tough games against the Philadelphia Phillies, another team in Pennsylvania.

Josh Harrison leaps to throw over a sliding Diamondbacks player. ➤

WHERE THEY PLAY

Beautiful PNC Park is where the Pirates play. Fans enjoy seeing the Pittsburgh **skyline** from their seats. They can also see the bright yellow Roberto Clemente Bridge. It was named for one of the team's greatest players. PNC Park opened in 2001. It is one of the smallest MLB ballparks. Nearly 39,000 fans can fit inside.

◄ *Tall buildings in Pittsburgh tower in the distance behind PNC Park.*

THE BASEBALL FIELD

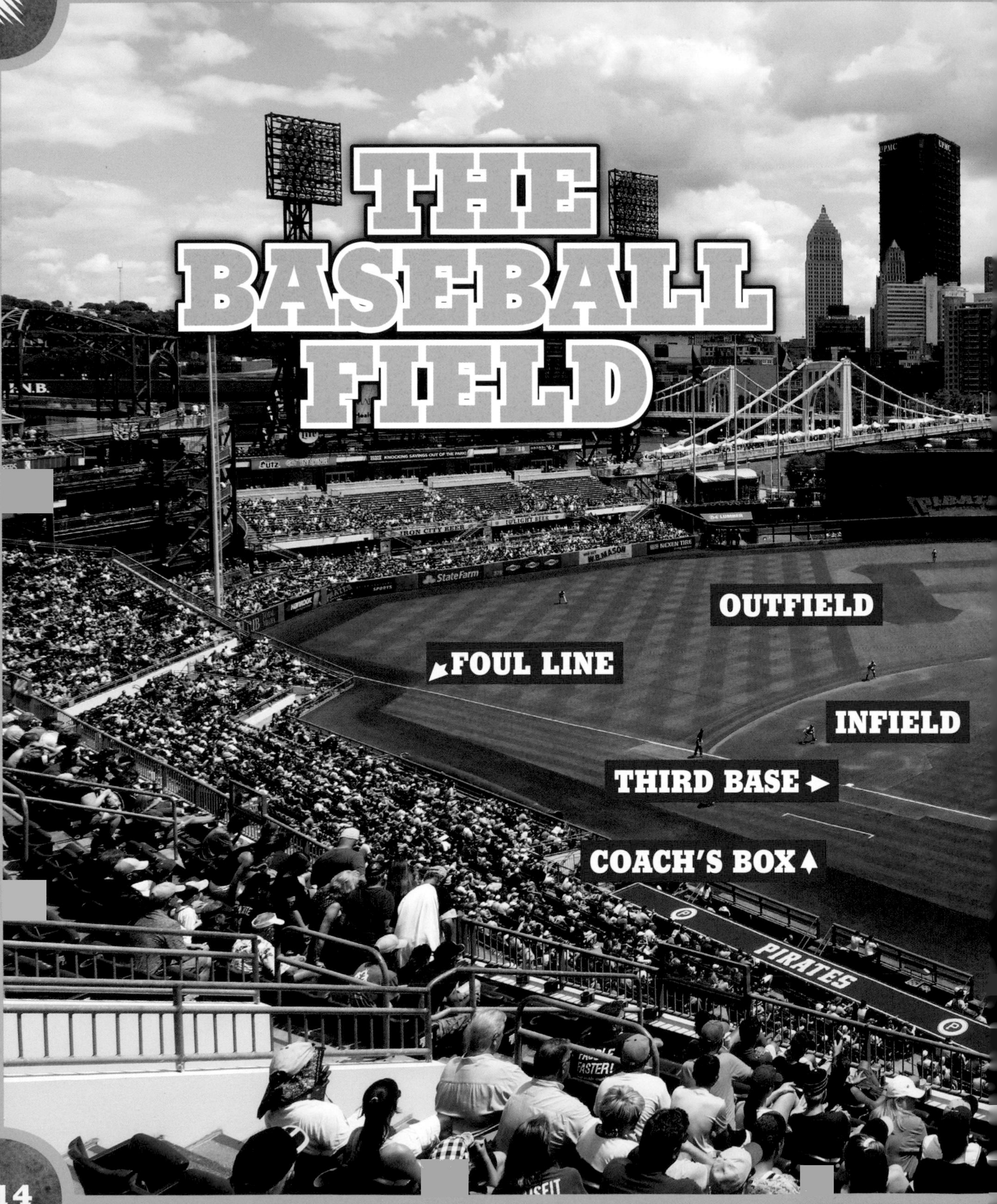

OUTFIELD

FOUL LINE

INFIELD

THIRD BASE ►

COACH'S BOX ▲

FOUL LINE

SECOND BASE

FIRST BASE

PITCHER'S MOUND

HOME PLATE

DUGOUT

ON-DECK CIRCLE

BIG DAYS

The Pirates have had a lot of great days in their long history. Here are a few of them.

1960—Pittsburgh shocked the mighty New York Yankees in the World Series. Most fans expected the Yankees to win. The Pirates played well, though. The Series was tied at 3 to 3. In the bottom of the ninth in Game 7, Bill Mazeroski hit a famous homer. The **walk-off hit** won the game and the Series!

1971—Led by the great Roberto Clemente, the Pirates won another World Series. They beat the Baltimore Orioles.

2013—After struggling for many years, the Pirates had a great team this year. Led by NL MVP Andrew McCutchen, the Pirates earned the wild-card spot! It was their first **playoff** game since 1992!

▼ *Bill Mazeroski (holding helmet) is chased by fans as he runs to score the winning run in 1960.*

TOUGH DAYS

Like every team, the Pirates have had some not-so-great days, too. Here are a few their fans might not want to recall.

1952—The Pirates have had some pretty bad teams. The worst one in the 20th century came this year, when they lost 112 games!

2010—The Pirates have lost a lot of games. On April 22 this year, they had their worst loss ever. They were beaten by the Milwaukee Brewers 20-0!

2015—Max Scherzer of the Washington Nationals showed the Pirates why he's an **ace**. He threw a **no-hitter** against them!

Milwaukee's Prince Fielder clubbed a homer ➤
when his team beat the Pirates in 2010.

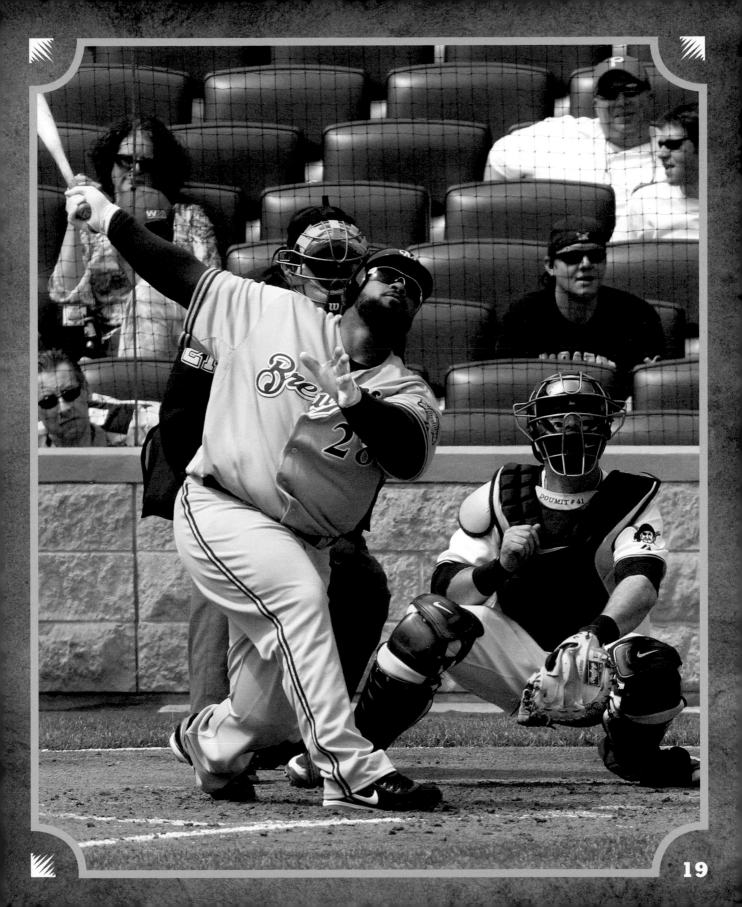

MEET THE FANS!

Pirates fans are patient and loyal! They went more than 20 seasons between seeing their team in the playoffs. They have also waited more than 40 years for another World Series title. They have some help cheering. The Pirate Parrot joined the team as the mascot in 1979. His silly act entertains fans at PNC Park.

Why a parrot? Because pirates love to have them around! Arr! ➤

HEROES THEN

The Pirates have had some amazing players. Baseball experts call Honus Wagner the best shortstop ever. He was a great hitter and base-stealer. Lloyd and Paul Waner were brothers who both made the Hall of Fame. Roberto Clemente was a hero to people in Pittsburgh and his native Puerto Rico. Willie "Pops" Stargell helped the Pirates win two World Series titles.

◄ *Roberto Clemente had exactly 3,000 hits in his Hall of Fame career.*

HEROES NOW

Today's Pirates have several great young players. Starling Marte combines speed and power to lead the team in hitting. Josh Harrison is a slugging first baseman. Jordy Mercer has been the team's starting shortstop for several seasons. On the mound, Ivan Nova is the staff ace. Young pitcher Jameson Taillon has the talent to become a big star.

Starling Marte has stolen more than 30 bases in five seasons. ➤

GEARING UP

Baseball players wear team uniforms. On defense, they wear leather gloves to catch the ball. As batters, they wear hard helmets. This protects them from pitches. Batters hit the ball with long wood bats. Each player chooses his own size of bat. Catchers have the toughest job. They wear a lot of protection.

THE BASEBALL

The outside of the Major League baseball is made from cow leather. Two leather pieces shaped like 8's are stitched together. There are 108 stitches of red thread. These stitches help players grip the ball. Inside, the ball has a small center of cork and rubber. Hundreds of feet of yarn are tightly wound around this center.

CATCHER'S MASK
← AND HELMET

CHEST
PROTECTOR →

▲ CATCHER'S
MITT

▲ SHIN GUARDS

CATCHER'S GEAR

TEAM STATS

Here are some of the all-time career records for the Pittsburgh Pirates. All these stats are through the 2018 regular season.

STRIKEOUTS

Bob Friend	1,682
Bob Veale	1,652

HITS

Roberto Clemente	3,000
Honus Wagner	2,967

BATTING AVERAGE

Jake Stenzel	.360
Paul Waner	.340

STOLEN BASES

Max Carey	688
Honus Wagner	639

WINS

Wilbur Cooper	202
Babe Adams	194
Sam Leever	194

SAVES

Roy Face	186
Kent Tekulve	158

Willie Stargell played 21 seasons for Pittsburgh. ➤

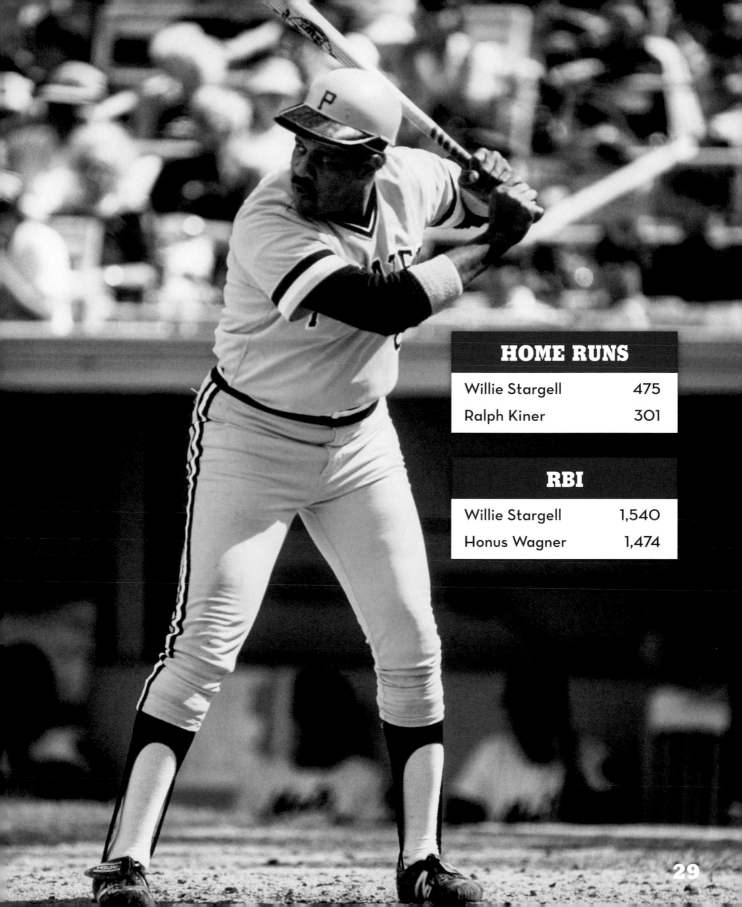

HOME RUNS

Willie Stargell	475
Ralph Kiner	301

RBI

Willie Stargell	1,540
Honus Wagner	1,474

GLOSSARY

ace (AYS) a team's top pitcher

no-hitter (no-HIT-er) a game in which a starting pitcher does not allow a single hit to the opponent

pennant (PEN-nunt) a thin, pointed flag; it represents the winning team in the AL or NL each year

playoff (PLAY-off) a game held after a regular season

rivals (RYE-vuhls) two people or groups competing for the same thing

skyline (SKY-lyn) the shape formed by a collection of tall buildings in a city

walk-off hit (WAWK-off HIT) a hit that immediately ends a game for the winning team

World Series (WURLD SEER-eez) the championship of Major League Baseball, played between the winners of the AL and NL

FIND OUT MORE

IN THE LIBRARY

Buckley, James Jr. *Who Was Roberto Clemente?*
New York, NY: Penguin Workshop, 2014.

Connery-Boyd, Peg. *Pittsburgh Pirates: The Big Book of Activities*. Chicago, IL: Sourcebooks/Jabberwocky, 2016.

Kortemeier, Todd. *12 Reasons to Love the Pittsburgh Pirates*. Mankato, MN: 12-Story Library, 2016

ON THE WEB

Visit our website for links about the Pittsburgh Pirates:
childsworld.com/links

Note to Parents, Teachers, and Librarians: We routinely verify our Web links to make sure they are safe and active sites. So encourage your readers to check them out!

INDEX